Perritos/Dogs

Poodles/
Poodles

por/by Lisa Trumbauer

Traducción/Translation: Dr. Martín Luis Guzmán Ferrer
Editor Consultor/Consulting Editor: Dra. Gail Saunders-Smith

Consultor/Consultant: Jennifer Zablotny, DVM
Member, American Veterinary Medical Association

Capstone press

Mankato, Minnesota

Pebble is published by Capstone Press,
151 Good Counsel Drive, P.O. Box 669, Mankato, Minnesota 56002.
www.capstonepress.com

1 2 3 4 5 6 13 12 11 10 09 08

Library of Congress Cataloging-in-Publication Data
Trumbauer, Lisa, 1963–
      [Poodles. Spanish & English]
      Poodles / por Lisa Trumbauer = Poodles / by Lisa Trumbauer.
      p. cm. — (Pebble. Perritos = Pebble. Dogs)
      ISBN-13: 978-1-4296-2385-8 (hardcover)
      ISBN-10: 1-4296-2385-3 (hardcover)
      1. Poodles — Juvenile literature. I. Title. II. Series.
SF429.P85T7818 2009
636.72'8 — dc22
                                                                2008001260

Summary: Simple text and photographs present an introduction to the poodle breed,
its growth from puppy to adult, and pet care information — in both English
and Spanish.

Note to Parents and Teachers

The Perritos/Dogs set supports national science standards related
to life science. This book describes and illustrates poodles in
both English and Spanish. The images support early readers in
understanding the text. The repetition of words and phrases helps
early readers learn new words. This book also introduces early
readers to subject-specific vocabulary words, which are defined
in the Glossary section. Early readers may need assistance to read
some words and to use the Table of Contents, Glossary, Internet
Sites, and Index sections of the book.

Table of Contents

Tabla de contenidos

4

Show Dogs

Poodles are show dogs.
Poodles with fancy haircuts
compete against other dogs
in dog shows.

Perros de exposición

Los poodles son perros
de exposición. Los poodles,
con elegantes cortes de pelo,
compiten contra otros perros
en las exposiciones.

Poodles work hard at
dog shows. They jump
and do tricks.

Los poodles trabajan duro
en las exposiciones de
perros. Saltan y hacen
toda clase de gracias.

From Puppy to Adult

Three to five puppies

are born in each

poodle litter.

De cachorro a adulto

Los poodles tienen de

tres a cinco cachorros

en cada camada.

Poodle puppies are smart. They play and learn together as they grow.

Los cachorros poodle son listos. Juegan y aprenden juntos mientras crecen.

Adult poodles come in three sizes. Toy poodles are small. Standard poodles are big. Miniature poodles are in between.

Hay tres tamaños de poodles adultos. Los poodle juguete son pequeñitos. Los poodles estándar son grandes. Los poodles miniatura son medianos.

Poodle Care

Poodles need dog food, fresh water, and walks every day.

Cómo cuidar a los poodles

Los poodles necesitan comida de perro, agua limpia y paseos todos los días.

A poodle's curly fur
is always growing.
Poodles need haircuts
every two months.

El pelo rizado de
los poodles siempre está
creciendo. Los poodles
necesitan un corte de pelo
cada dos meses.

Poodle fur can get
matted and tangled.
Owners must brush
their poodles often.

El pelo del poodle se
puede enredar y hacerse
nudos. Los dueños deben
cepillar a menudo a
sus poodles.

Poodles are smart, active dogs. Love and care make poodles happy pets.

Los poodles son perros listísimos y muy activos. El cariño y los cuidados hacen que los poodles sean felices.

Glossary

compete — to try hard to do better than others at a task, race, or contest

dog show — a contest where judges pick the best dog in several events

litter — a group of animals born at one time to the same mother

matted — stuck together

tangled — twisted together in a confused group

Internet Sites

FactHound offers a safe, fun way to find Internet sites related to this book. All of the sites on FactHound have been researched by our staff.

Here's how:

1. Visit *www.facthound.com*
2. Choose your grade level.
3. Type in this book ID **1429623853** for age-appropriate sites. You may also browse subjects by clicking on letters, or by clicking on pictures and words.
4. Click on the **Fetch It** button.

FactHound will fetch the best sites for you!

22

Glosario

la camada — grupo de recién nacidos que la hembra tiene al mismo tiempo

competir — esforzarse por hacer las cosas mejor que otros en una tarea, carrera o competencia

enredado — retorcido entre sí formando un grupo desordenado

la exposición de perros — concurso donde los jueces escoben al mejor perro en una serie de competencias

hacerse nudos — apelmazarse entre sí

Sitios de Internet

FactHound te brinda una manera divertida y segura de encontrar sitios de Internet relacionados con este libro. Hemos investigado todos los sitios de FactHound. Es posible que algunos sitios no estén en español.

Se hace así:

1. Visita *www.facthound.com*

2. Elige tu grado escolar.

3. Introduce este código especial **1429623853** para ver sitios apropiados a tu edad, o usa una palabra relacionada con este libro para hacer una búsqueda general.

4. Haz un clic en el botón **Fetch It**.

¡FactHound buscará los mejores sitios para ti!

Index

Índice

Editorial Credits

Martha E. H. Rustad, editor; Katy Kudela, bilingual editor; Adalín Torres-Zayas, Spanish copy editor; Juliette Peters, designer; Kelly Garvin, photo researcher; Scott Thoms, photo editor

Photo Credits

Ardea/Jean Paul Ferrero, 8; Cheryl A. Ertelt, 18; Corbis/Tom Stewart, 20; Elite Portrait Design/Lisa Fallenstein-Holthaus, 14, 16; Kent Dannen, cover, 10, 12; Mark Raycroft, 1; Mira/Karen Stewart, 6; Zuma Press/Baron Catskill, 4

24